THE WAY IT WAS
ON OLDE CAPE COD

OTHER PUBLICATIONS

Boys and Girls on Olde Cape Cod
Indians on Olde Cape Cod
Sketches of Old Cape Cod
Craigville on Old Cape Cod
Churches on Cape Cod
Along the Wampanoag Trail
America's Religious Treasures
Cape Cod in Color
Martha's Vineyard in Color
Meditations By The Sea

THE WAY IT WAS
ON OLDE CAPE COD

The history, personality and way of life of early settlers, earning a living on Olde Cape Cod

by
MARION RAWSON VUILLEUMIER

Reprinted with permission of
The Cape Cod Times

Illustrations by Louis Edward Vuilleumier

The Butterworth Company
23 Traders Lane
West Yarmouth, Massachusetts 02673

TO MY HUSBAND

PREFACE

Since civilization began man has been involved with wresting a living from his environment. Some have found this easier and more satisfying than others. History shows that honest toil has been a help rather than a detriment in the search for personal happiness. Abraham Lincoln commented "If ever this people is utterly demoralized, it will come from this human struggle for a way to live without work."

Our Cape Cod predecessors were involved in all sorts of work. Early Plymouth records show men busy as millers, blacksmiths, planters, carpenters, shoemakers, feltmakers, sheriffs and cowkeepers. In the census of 1850 sailmakers, coopers, wheelwrights, harness makers and lighthouse keepers were at work. By 1892 mariners, surfmen, factory workers and merchants had appeared. In fairly recent memory there have been lamp lighters, shellfish constables and regulators of the herring brook. Our forebears certainly adjusted to changing times, creating new jobs when old ones ceased.

A study of the ways Cape Codders earned a living a century and more ago, reveals the history, personality and environment of the early residents. This seems reason enough to add another book to the many already written about Cape Cod.

A special thank you is due to all who helped by interviews and by providing research material thereby making this book as accurate as possible.

CONTENTS

PAGE

THE GREAT SKIN GAME (Tannery) 1

AUTOMATION CAUSED A RIOT (Glass Works) . . . 5

THE MOST ESSENTIAL MAN IN TOWN (Mills) . . . 11

SALT FROM THE SEA (Saltworks) 15

RAISE THE BARREL — PACKET'S COMIN' (Packets) . . 20

STAGECOACHES COME TO CAPE COD (Stagecoaches) . 25

THE INDUSTRY THAT VANISHED (Fulling Mills) . . . 30

ARE THEY LOGS OR FISH? (Fishing) 37

WHEN FARMERS WERE WHALERS (Off Shore Whaling) 42

GOLD STRIKE IN THE BOGS (Cranberries) 48

IRON FROM THE SWAMPS (Iron Works) 53

FROM METROPOLIS TO GHOST TOWN (Car Works) . 57

KEEPERS OF THE ORDINARY! (Innkeeping) 63

THE THREE R'S ON OLD CAPE COD (Schoolteaching) 70

BIBLIOGRAPHY 77

INDEX 79

THE GREAT SKIN GAME

About a century ago a native Cape Codder decided to get in to the skin game He wasn't a con man selling Highland Light to the gullible forerunners of today's tourists; rather he was a Cape Codder who decided to open a tannery.

Tanners weren't new in the Cape area. The Indians were well versed in the craft when the white men arrived on these shores. Usually the Indian women did the laborious work of removing hair and smoking the hides so their families would have garments to protect them from rain and snow.

The first tanner to arrive here was Experience Miller, who came to Plymouth in 1623. He brought with him the method of bark tanning, unknown to the Indians. Miller's training was with the English Guild, which had a thousand year history. In the new world, he immediately went to work on the skins and hides available.

The art of tanning grew and in the early 1800's great strides were made in the industry with discoveries of new tanning chemicals, and inventions of machinery to eliminate arduous hand labor. Machines were created to de-hair and scrape hides, and to split the skins in layers.

Edward Clark, an Eastham native who was working in a Boston tannery in the early 1800's, had a longing to live back home on Cape Cod. (Doesn't that sound familiar?) Finally the hankering grew so strong he decided to open his own tannery on land he owned bordering Great Pond in Eastham.

This decision brought him happily back to the Cape. He must have been a better tanner than business man, however, for most unhappily, he was immediately beset by a number of problems, mostly related to transportation.

Lumber for the tannery building had to come by packet boat from Boston. Unloaded at the shore, it was picked up by Myric Clark teamster, who brought the wood overland in his truck-wagon pulled by his faithful — but not speedy — horse Dolly. Eventually enough materials arrived over this uncertain route for a three story building which was erected at the pond's edge.

The transportation problems which began with the building, continued to make difficulties for Mr. Clark. All hides to be tanned had to be shipped down from Boston. All freight shipped out had to traverse this same uncertain route. Mr. Clark must have been relieved when the railroad finally made it to Orleans in 1865, some five years after the start of his business.

A second problem at the very start of the tannery was the training of workers. The tanning process was long and arduous and Cape labor was unskilled. Though eventually employees became knowledgeable in the work, the process remained tedious and slow, since Mr. Clark could not afford the latest in machinery.

Although some of the hair was removed from the hides before it arrived in Eastham, the rest had to be carefully removed as the first step in the tanning process. The hides were first soaked in large vats for several days. These vats were on the first floor of the tannery and were filled with water from the pond to which a tanning substance had been added. The hides were then taken to the next floor, spread out on long benches and rubbed with soapstone. This smoothed the leather and removed every hair. Two layers were then peeled off. Each layer was smoothed out and covered with fish, tallow, or olive oils. The Cape boys used to catch skate and mackerel to help with the oil supply. After the oil was rubbed in well, the leather was hung on racks for several days. All this was quite a process for Cape men to learn.

Mrs. B. H. McHenry of Springfield reports in an old newspaper article that her Grandfather Hatch had charge of the splitting machine. After the leather had absorbed the oils, her grandfather maneuvered the skins through the machine while a lad named Jimmy Boland turned the crank.

Some of the leather was colored by dye made of boiling water, log wood and lamp black. This was applied to the skins with a brush, and the product was called grain leather. Some was left a natural color and sold to James Boyd and Sons in Boston for fire hose. (This was before the days of rubber.) Grain leather was used for shoes, valises and carpet bags. There was a special pebble machine which was worked by hand and turned out pebble leather for shoes and harnesses. A man called a glosser finished the leather by smoothing it with a special tool made of glass.

The tanning factor was a boon to Eastham. It employed 25-30 men. According to Mrs. McHenry's account, "Wages were paid for a ten hour day and the pay was fixed according to the work done. The manager of the splitting machine received 30 cents an hour. The glosser was paid 25 cents an hour and the general utility man received 15 cents an hour. The lowest paid man owned his own home."

The factory may have been a boon to Eastham's economy but it was the opposite to Mr. Clark's finances. He continued to be plagued by problems. The overhead was too great. The crude manner of working and the lack of machinery made his output lag behind his competitors. Finally, after 15 years of operation, the owner closed the factory. Even the forces of nature seemed against him, for the building was blown down later by a high wind.

Other tanners are mentioned in early Cape records. In 1800 there was a small tannery at Old Harbor, owned by a Crosby who ground bark with a windmill. This enterprise lasted until 1831 when it was abandoned. The historian Frederick Freeman refers to tanners and curriers who worked on the Cape in the 16 and 17 hundreds. They existed as needed apparently as one or two man operations, going out of business when machines and inland factories evolved in the mid 1800's.

The records checked do not say whether Mr. Clark left his native Eastham shores after his business failure. Perhaps he settled down to enjoy life on the Cape living off the bounty of its woods, streams and oceans. Where else would a native Cape Codder be happy even though his skin game fell through?

AUTOMATION CAUSED A RIOT

The glass industry at Sandwich was famous for its intricate, lacy pieces, the first pressed glass, and its development of exquisite colors. A lesser known event makes it also noted as the first place automation threatened the workers of America.

Deming Jarves established the Boston Sandwich Glass Company on Cape Cod in 1824 because of the plentiful forests which were available to feed the hungry fires of the glass blowers. He also hoped to use the abundant sand in the seashore community. Ironically the Cape shore sands proved unsuitable to glass making and sand had to be shipped in from Morris River, New Jersey and later from the Berkshire Hills of Massachusetts. In spite of this difficulty the glass factory became successful. The company owned thousands of acres of forests. Its large yard was soon surrounded with homes built for the workmen, many of whom came from off Cape. The factory was very large and exceedingly well built, with a large cone shaped structure housing the furnaces.

About a century ago the industry employed 500 workers and had $500,000 invested in it. A large bell rang to signal the changes of shifts the volume of work demanded. Deming Jarves had managed to overcome most difficulties and had a smooth running operation. His one thorn in the flesh was the temperament of the glass blowers.

Since glass making was a new venture in this country, there were no native glass blowers. Experts in the art had

to be brought from Europe. They were interesting men who through their work had developed strong backs, fire-proof skins and lungs of leather. There was Gaffer Bonique, who it was hinted, was the lost Dauphine of France. Another was Rice Harris, who was brought over from England for six months at a cost of $5,000. These men blew intricate glass pieces and trained the first local workers. The elite employees at the factory were the glass blowers, and they let every one else know it.

Several years after the factory began, Deming Jarves saw one of his local employees experimenting with a wooden mould. "If we make a mould like this, pour in glass, and place a smaller mould just like it inside, we'd have glass without blowing," said the worker. Jarvis was immediately excited, visualizing the possibilities of this pressed glass. Mass production of pieces would sharply increase the output. Sets of identical pieces could be marketed at low cost. Prices would be low enough for the average person to buy glass. The business implications were tremendous.

The glass blowers uneasily visualized other possibilities. What would happen to their jobs if moulds formed the glass? They preserved an outward calm, however, watching the development of the moulds. They scoffed at the experiment. No one had ever heard of anything but blown glass. This was a crazy idea that wouldn't work, they derided.

Finally Jarves was ready to try the first pressed glass. The workers gathered around with interest, some in an ominous mood. They watched in silence as the moulten glass was poured into the outer mould and the inner mould was set in place. The glass was cooled, then the mould removed. A pressed glass tumbler emerged. Although the process had to be perfected, it was clear that dishes and glasses could be made without blowing. The men stood in stunned silence. Then the glass blowers growled. With a roar they started toward Jarves. This man was going to put them out of business!

Jarves snatched his mould and beat a hasty retreat. For several weeks he didn't go near the factory. Meanwhile he sent assurances that pressed glass would be an additional product, not a replacement for blown glass. Finally tempers cooled and work on the moulds began. The factory started production slowly, but eventually turned out one hundred thousand pounds of glass a week. This developed the use of another local product — salt hay. A Cape Codder recently commented that his mother packed glass at the old Sandwich factory sending tons of salt hay around our country and overseas.

The fame of the factory spread across the world. Russia once ordered 80 thousand dollars worth of lamps. The renown of the glass works also spread west across our own country as American companies placed orders of 100 thousand dollars worth at a time. This was the place where the huge Union Bowl was created for Daniel Webster. The mould for this took two men six months to create. Designs of extremely beautiful frosted lace appeared and the unique silver sheen on glass was produced.

The antagonism of the glass blowers never fully disappeared and tempers of the second generation elite flared just as easily. The workers organized a union in 1887 and were ready to strike on the first important issue. By this time Deming Jarves was no longer with the company. The management continued to be creative and adjusted as new methods appeared. The one problem they were having trouble overcoming was fuel to feed the furnaces. Cape Cod had been denuded of its trees and there was a desperate search on for better firing methods.

Unfortunately the antagonism of the workers flared up at this inopportune time, when one man received a smaller pay check than he expected. The Union struck and the officials gave up. The fires went out and the Cape lost an industry that was basic to its economy a century ago. Sandwich glass can now be seen on collectors' shelves or in bits and pieces set in jewelry. We are fortunate that much has been written about this industry, and that the Sandwich Glass Museum has preserved much historic information as well as a marvelous collection of the glass that made Sandwich famous.

THE MOST ESSENTIAL MAN IN TOWN

Who is the most essential man in town? In today's complex and interdependent society this question is a poser. A century or more ago the answer was easy — the miller!

Corn was the basis of survival of the early Cape Codders. This "yellow gold" was the principal food as well as the first currency. Some wheat was raised, but an early blight stopped it from being a major crop. No one had much money but everyone could raise corn. With this staple our ancestors paid the ministers, bought their farms, purchased animals and fed their families.

The first settlers raised their corn without difficulty thanks to the help of friendly Indians. They had a real problem grinding any quantity however, for home hand mortars required much energy and produced little meal. The nearest grist mill to the Cape was at Plymouth and that was a long way even from Sandwich. Cape residents soon determined to build their own mills.

A mill builder, or millwright, was hard to find. This was an art as difficult as shipbuilding. The early mill-wrights (unnamed) were imported, however, and soon the streams in Falmouth, Bourne, Sandwich, Barnstable and Brewster were merrily powering grist mills.

Later on windmills were built, mostly by Thomas Paine of Eastham, who traveled from town to town in answer to good sized material rewards. Another family of mill-wrights was the Baxter clan of West Yarmouth. The Baxter men built a grist mill in 1710 and their descendants ran the mill for almost 200 years. Other times the builders moved on and a townsman became the miller. Such a one was Henry Hall, who left a seagoing career to become a miller in Dennis.

The miller was so important to the town that great inducements were offered to secure one. The mill was untaxed and the miller himself was exempt from taxation. He was also excluded from military service and was given land next to the mill for his home. He occupied high social position and was a man of influence in town affairs. His wages were paid by a stated quantity to be retained from each bushel ground. This was known as the "miller's pottle".

Like all jobs of importance, responsibility went with it. The miller had to turn out each man's corn with as little delay as possible. He had to be exact in measuring so he wouldn't be called a "pottle stretcher". The running of the mill was an exacting task also. If the mill was powered by wind, he had to climb the long arms and set the sails in nautical fashion each morning. At night he must climb up and unfurl them. If the wind blew hard he had to shorten sail. In a gale the mill ran with no sail furled. In addition, he had to adjust the mill's tail according to the wind direction. Many millers needed to be retired seamen who had learned climbing on Cape Schooners.

At times the job was dangerous. Once 70 year old Henry Hall stopped his mill to shorten sail but he neglected to make the arms taut with the huge iron chain. When he was half way up one arm they all began to turn. With amazing agility the old seaman worked his way down to the shaft, which was revolving. Here he perched three stories high. He kept upright by hitching himself up and down as the shaft turned. The old miller was exhausted when help came.

If the mill was water powered there were other problems. In winter the miller had to stop the ice from forming. This made the paddles run unevenly and caused the building and mechanism to wobble. If solid ice formed, the wheel was useless. Also, the amount of power available depended on the water backed up in the pond. There wasn't much grinding in a dry year. No wonder the underwater turbine was added to the West Yarmouth mill in 1860.

The miller worked long hours with no union to keep him on an eight hour day. According to Oliver Evans in "The Young Millwright and Miller's Guide" printed in 1800, the miller must sweep the floor then nail, weigh, mark and brand the casks, sharpen the grinding stones, and keep the mechanism in excellent shape. All this was in addition to regulating the feed and water (or wind) during the actual grinding process. Some mills continued grinding through the night, having two millers on duty in shifts.

In the early 1800's there were between 30 and 40 mills on the Cape. One of the most interesting (and well traveled) was the Farris mill which was built on the north side of the Cape. Reuben Farris stayed in Fall River all that winter waiting for the Run stone. He brought it to the Cape by ship and it took 14 yoke of oxen to drag the six thousand pound stone to the mill.

Its next move was to South Yarmouth, then in 1782 the old mill was moved to Indian Town, later called Friends'

Village, by Samuel Farris and David Kelley. William Kenney, a descendant of Samuel Farris described the move as a gala occasion when the whole village turned out to see the curious shaped structure with the giant arms roll by on green pine wood from which the bark had been stripped. After the tired and thirsty movers enjoyed refreshment, they set the arms awhirling to celebrate.

Later the mill was fixed on its permanent foundation and the rumble of the grinding stone and the cog wheel greeted the teams of oxen and the men and women afoot who brought grain and departed with grist.

When its usefulness as a mill ended it was purchased by Mr. F. A. Abell and put on his West Yarmouth property in 1894. Later it traveled again, this time to Henry Ford's Dearborn Village where it stands today reminding visitors of old Cape Cod.

Through the hoppers and down between the stones of these early mills flowed the corn which came out as delicious meal. Wheat was also ground to some extent, resulting in flour that makes one's mouth water in retrospect. During a Cape summer people may see the remains of this old industry by visiting the old mill at Brewster, the restored mill in West Yarmouth and the windmill at Orleans. At the watermill in Sandwich visitors can watch the old process then buy the stone ground products, enabling them to bake muffins and bread with the old time flavor. One can see why some modern bread companies still buy flour from commercially operated grist mills.

A century has made a difference on the Cape though. The miller as a man of importance has receded into history. He's not essential. He's not even here. Yet this was one way a few Cape Codders earned a living on old Cape Cod.

SALT FROM THE SEA

With current water shortage nearing disaster stages in some areas, the nations of the world are putting their best scientific minds to the problem of removing the salt from the ocean. Only recently Israel allocated a small fortune to build a fresh water-making plant at the ocean side to feed its thirsty desert. Cape Codders began this process over two hundred years ago but their end product was not fresh water but salt.

The business of making salt from sea water with nature supplying the raw materials and the evaporating power, appealed to thrifty Cape Codders. According to Gertrude DeWager who wrote for the Provincetown Advocate in 1941, the early fishermen needed salt to preserve their large fish catches until they could bring them to market. Imported salt was expensive because of the taxes. Thus Cape Mariners couldn't overlook the salt water at their front doors.

At first salt was taken from the sea in primitive fashion. Sea water was brought from the shore in buckets, poured into wooden vats and left in the sun to evaporate. Some hastened the process by boiling the water in large tubs. Thus Cape forests were substantially reduced. Either process was slow and tedious for it took 400 gallons of sea water to produce one bushel of salt.

In 1776 Captain John Sears of Dennis took note of the high price of salt due to the British blockade, and of the bounty of three shillings offered by the General Court for

salt locally made from seawater. Using his nautical knowledge, he built tight water vats and following a suggestion from Major Freeman of Harwich, drew his water from the ocean with a windmill.

Other Cape Cod inventors went to work. Reuben Sears of Harwich in 1793 constructed a roof that could cover the salt vats when the weather was bad, and could be removed when the sun shone. Then Hallil Kelly of Dennis refined the roof scheme so that two roofs were balanced on one central pole. These could be pivoted over and off the vats when necessary.

Salt making sprang almost immediately into a major Cape industry. James Freeman reports in 1802 that 136 separate salt works were producing over 40,000 bushels of salt and 182,000 bushels of Glauber salt — a medicinal by-product. In the 1830's the peak of the industry was reached. There were 442 individual works with an average output of half a million bushels — not counting salt by-products.

Henry Kittredge in his book "Cape Cod, Its People and Their History" says that Loring Crocker's establishment at the Common Fields in Barnstable was the finest example of salt making. Mr. Crocker laid his log pipes to the low water mark and built his wooden reservoirs on the ridge of the beach. Mr. Crocker's process of salt making as described by Kittredge is fascinating. The water was run by waterfalls through seven vats, each built lower than the other. These vats were 18 by 50 or 60 feet and 1 foot deep. The first three, called water rooms, took out the vegetation and evaporated the liquid. In the second group of three vats, called pickle rooms, lime was precipitated and remained on the bottom while the water flowed into the last vat, called the salt room. Here the residue remained until salt crystalized and was shoveled into storage sheds to dry. Some was ground for table salt while most was left in its present state for use as a preservative. The whole process took six weeks more or less, depending on the weather.

The by-products of this industry were several. The "bitter water" which was left when ordinary salt was removed, was used for making Epsom Salts. Some of the bitter water was also used for making a special cement used in filigree work. Glauber Salts were sold to tanneries and used to allow hides to dry slowly.

A great deal of the Cape prosperity in the 1830's was directly due to the salt industry. At one time two million dollars of Cape money was invested and the return on the investment was 25 per cent.

One old Cape Codder writing in the Cape Cod Magazine of September 1915 recalls rows and rows of the salt vats on his grandparents' farm. According to him, women's home duties included tending the salt vats as well as housekeeping, bringing water from the well and tending the animals. He recalls as a child going with his grandmother and several small brothers and sisters to put the roofs over the salt vats at sunset time. The creaking of the roof turning machinery could be heard all over the village as the vats were closed before the rains came.

The elements could play havoc with this industry. In addition to the fickleness of the sunshine, there are accounts of storms causing great losses. One gale in Provincetown in 1838 swept 20 salt mills into the sea.

In 1840 the industry began to decline, for mined salt from other areas become cheaper. In 1837, in Barnstable for example, there were 34 salt establishments. By 1845 there were only 24, while by 1865 only three were still active. Salt works in other Cape towns decreased as rapidly. The historian Deyo says that the industry finally became extinct around 1888 when the arms of the salt mills along the shore of Bass River ceased to turn.

The old works lay abandoned, but the lumber was sometimes reclaimed by thrifty Cape Codders. Carpenters whose tools became rusty after a few days labor with this wood, weren't sure this was a saving.

According to the American People's Encyclopedia, the water in some of the United States communities is reaching a dangerous low. In time this supply may become exhausted. In Louisville, Kentucky for example, the underwater ground level has dropped 40 feet in ten years. When 65,000 gallons are needed to produce one ton of steel, and 800,000 gallons are needed to irrigate a one acre orange grove, our dependency on water becomes more apparent. Ocean water is our great, largely untapped resource. Scientists are very much aware of the need for new processes to tap this supply. One wonders if some day the Cape, projected as it is out into this vast reservoir, may again be the scene of an industry developed to separate the salt from the sea.

RAISE THE BARREL — PACKETS COMIN!

The most colorful of the early Cape Cod occupations were with the Packet Boats that kept residents in touch with the outside world. After homes were established, crops growing and mills operating, Cape men turned to boat building, for water was the easiest channel to Boston, New York and the great cities of the world. The overland journey by foot, horseback or stagecoach was long and arduous, for roads were crude, streams had to be forded and bridges were poorly constructed. It's no wonder that people preferred to travel by boat. Henry Kittredge tells us that most wise men on the Cape knew their way by sea to China, better than by land to Boston. Also, it was much easier for farmers on the Cape's north shore to ship their produce fifty miles by water to Boston, than three miles to the south shore over land. Cagy Cape Codders took note of these needs and built a thriving business of benefit to the Cape for over 150 years.

The first Packets ran intermittently. According to Donald Trayser in "Three Centuries a Cape Cod Town", Thomas Huckins of Barnstable was one of the first Packet Masters. He was also Tavern Keeper, Constable, Selectman, Surveyor, Deputy, Fisherman, Farmer and Collector of the Excises. In 1663 Excise Collector Huckins reports taxes paid by Packet Master Huckins on 179 gallons of spirits plus powder and shot brought from Boston mostly for Tavern Keeper Huckins! According to the historian Deyo, one of the first packets was the "Charming Betty" which began its Boston-Sandwich run in 1717. In 1794

Rev. John Mellen, Pastor of the East Precinct Church (now the Unitarian Church of Barnstable) writes that the towns yearly produced between 12-18 thousand bushels of onions as well as corn, flaxseed, rye, codfish and salt. All this was shipped to Boston by Packet.

By the early 1800's most Cape towns had several packets which were comfortable staunch and speedy. By 1820 the business was brisk all over the Cape, but its peak was reached in the 1840's. Trayser lists twenty-one packets active just out of Barnstable between 1806 and 1858. South shore packets ran from Hyannis, Cotuit, Centerville, Osterville and Falmouth to Nantucket, New Bedford, New York and sometimes the Rhode Island and Connecticut shores. North Side Packets went regularly to Boston in about seven hours time at a cost of $1.50 round trip. Activity ceased only in mid-winter.

The Packets were a boon to the Cape economy for in addition to passenger and freight service, they brought business to the sail maker, rigger, builder, and chandler (supplier). In addition harbor workers, crewmen, stewards and captains were needed.

These Packets were nautical schools, for many boys who began coiling rope at dockside, ended their careers on the quarter-decks of Clipper ships on the other side of the globe. Although the first Packets were small, later ones like the "Post Boy" of Truro, which was the belle of the bay for many years, were magnificent. The "Post Boy's" cabin was finished in birds-eye maple and she had draperies made of silk. She was described as the "finest specimen of naval architecture and passenger accommodation ever seen in Cape waters". Sandwich was always well serviced with Packets, due largely to the needs of the Sand-

21

wich Glass Co. In 1825 the "Polly" was a town Packet, later rivaled by the "Sandwich" built by the Glass works. Great rivalry existed through the years between town and factory Packets.

All Cape Codders loved a boat race just as the present ones do today. Many rivalries sprang up within and between the towns. When one Cape town had the last word in Packets, another town soon set out to top it. In 1828 Yarmouth owned the finest and fastest sloop on the coast — the "Commodore Hull". The ship would sail past anything afloat and beat everyone's time to Boston. Barnstable citizens could only stand this so long. Then Captains Matthias Hinckley and Thomas Percival, backed by Daniel Bacon commissioned the sloop "Mail" from a boat company on the Hudson. There was great excitement in 1837 when the "Mail" arrived for its first trip against the "Commodore Hull".

They sailed side by side for Boston, leaving behind two wildly excited towns and many a wager. They came into Central Wharf at Boston Harbor just six hours later, still side by side, but with the "Mail" three lengths ahead. Apparently it wasn't a clear victory, however, for two Captains were on the "Mail" while only one, Captain Thomas Matthews was on the "Commodore Hull".

Packet Boats were social institutions for early Cape people. When 25-50 individuals were in such close quarters for a day there was much feasting and talk. Packet Lines hired good stewards for they knew sea air increased appetites. For twenty-five cents one could get a plain but sizable meal. Meanwhile the talk would range, says Deyo, from "original sin to the price of cod-fish". A copy of a bill for passengers and merchandise made out by the Barnstable Packet Line in 1830 reads as follows:

Lothrop Davis Dr. to Schooner Sappho

1 Passage to Boston	$1.00
1 Passage home, yourself, meal	1.17
1 Passage home wife and child	1.50
1 Bedstead, 1 Demijohn Ink, 1 Tub Sugar, Soap, Pail and bundle	.59
1 Barrel Flour and 1 Barrel Books	.37
	$4.63

The Packets also carried the mail. When the ship neared home, a barrel was raised on the flag pole of the highest hill to alert the community. By the time it docked, there was always a sizable crowd on hand to welcome friends, pick up freight, check for mail, or just hear the news. When a long awaited seaman was aboard it was a gala day. Trayser tells us that one Sunday in 1840 the "Globe" arrived at Barnstable all decked with flags. Most of the village rushed down to see who was coming and remained to greet Elisha Loring, eldest son of Edward, who was returning after many years in Valpariso.

The Captains of these vessels must occasionally have been extremely frustrated. Not only did the weather sometimes make havoc of their schedules, but sailing and arrival times were always dependent upon the tides. At Barnstable shore when the Packet was ready to sail on the next tide a flag was raised on "Barrell Hill". We can imagine the prospective traveler climbing up to his Captain's walk with his telescope to keep an eye on the flag pole, the Packet and the tide. Williard DeLue, writing about Orleans in the newspaper, says the Packet boats could only come into Orleans Harbor on full tide and dared not be caught in between tides or the vessel would keel over on its side. He says that heavily loaded coal boats would come in as far as they could on the high tide, then when the tide went out, men would go over the flats with horses to remove part of the cargo. The lightened ship could then sail in on the next full tide.

The Railroads, which arrived in 1848 sounded the death knell of the Packets. Progress always steps on someone's toes, it is said. Thus these gallant colorful ships were swallowed up by the belching iron monsters. Yet graceful private yachts, excursion steamers, government ships, and the perennial fishing boats that abound in Cape waters, remind us of the vivid and vigorous Packet fleet of long ago.

STAGECOACHES COME TO CAPE COD

Airplanes haven't been the only conveyances that deposit the traveler at one place and his luggage at another. Joseph C. Lincoln, as he reminisces in "Cape Cod Yesterdays" tells of a couple's arrival home by stagecoach from Boston in the midst of a blinding snowstorm after a long trip at sea. When the coach arrived at its destination, the snow covered driver climbed down and said "Here ye are, part of ye anyway." "Part of us?" queried the travelers. "The strap broke and your trunk fell off" was the answer. Since this was the trunk that held presents for all the home folks, you can imagine the anguish that ensued. The next morning a Dennis resident found the trunk upended in a drift. Since it was tagged and labelled, he hailed the next stagecoach and lifted it on. The trunk was delivered later that day with presents intact — to the relief of the youngsters in the family.

A few stagecoaches arrived in America in the late 16 Hundreds, but the first regular run was in 1760, from New York to Philadelphia in "the flying machine, a good stage wagon on springs".

Cape residents made do with boat and horseback transportation until almost 1800. A few used a curious conveyance called the sedan chair. Alice Earle in her book "Home Life in Colonial America" recalls a notation about Cape Cod in Judge Sewall's diary reading "Five Indians carried Mr. Bromfield in a chair." Some affluent residents owned horses and carriages. A few hired rigs when needed.

Finally in 1790 the first regular run began when a stage-coach lumbered from Plymouth to Sandwich.

One of the most energetic men to earn his living by stage driving was William Boyden who in 1820 regularly left Sandwich early in the morning and made a round trip to Falmouth and Plymouth in one day. After three months this schedule was too much for him and he was obliged to keep the run to Plymouth, turning the Falmouth run to another driver. It was about this time that the mail bags were sent in stagecoaches rather than by horseback with the post riders.

The Boston Barnstable run began in 1830, according to Donald Trayser in "Three Centuries a Cape Cod Town". The stagecoach poster read "The Mail Stage starts from Captain W. Chipman's stage house opposite the court house, at half past 3 in the morning daily (Sundays excepted) for Boston. Arrives usually at or near 6 o'clock, Sundays excepted." Residents of Yarmouth and Hyannis had to arise at 2 A.M. to make this stage. Trayser tells us that the coach paused in Sandwich for breakfast, Plymouth for dinner and reached Boston for supper. The trip cost $5.00 and when business was brisk, nine persons rode wedged together rather uncomfortably.

Growth in stagecoach travel in the east came with the development of the "turnpikes" The first of these marvelous new roads was opened in 1792 between Philadelphia and Lancaster, Pa. These turnpikes soon spread to all the major cities of the northeast. In 1838 Pennsylvania alone had 2500 miles of turnpikes costing 37 million dollars. In 1827 the Traveler's Register in Boston lists 800 stage-coaches arriving in Boston and as many departing in one week. The 40 mile road from Boston to Providence sometimes had 20 coaches going each way. The Editor of the Providence Gazette wrote of the trip, "We were rattled from Boston to Providence in four hours and fifty minutes and if anyone wants to go faster he may go to Kentucky and charter a Streak of lightening."

All this had an effect on the Cape and before long stage lines criss-crossed the peninsular reaching as far as Provincetown. Many and colorful were the Cape Codders who earned their living by driving stage. Captain John F. Cornish of Centerville was the "whip" who for 12 years ran a line which left his village at 1 A.M., went to Hyannis for mail at 2, then on to Osterville, Marstons Mills, Cotuit and South Sandwich, where at 7 A.M. it connected with the Boston Stage. Intrepid Charley Howard on the Barnstable run was known for dashing his team up Meeting House Hill at full speed no matter what the weather. Other equally colorful but unnamed characters would jog quietly along most of the trip, but whip up the horses to full speed at journey's end, dramatically tearing up to the stage house on time to the second (even if they had to wait at the edge of town a few minutes to make the time just right).

Stagecoaches, like the Packet boats, were great equalizing and democratic influences. Men of all stations and degree on the social scale were in very close proximity all day. The long ride gave ample opportunity for an exchange of views and news, while the rest stops at various taverns along the way made the company increasingly congenial.

Cape travelers jogged from Cornishes in South Plymouth to Fessenden's in Sandwich, then on to Howlands in West Barnstable. After this there was a stop at Crockers' in Barnstable and Sears in Yarmouth. By the time spirits were tasted in all these places none knew or cared if the road was tortuous and hard!

Stage travel was not smooth and easy. Sometimes passengers were called on to push when the wheels sank almost hub deep in Cape sand. A traveler called Weld in 1795 says that the driver frequently had to call on the passengers in the stage to lean out of the carriage first on one side and then on the other to prevent it from over-setting in the deep ruts with which the road abounds. "Now, gentlemen to the right," the driver would call and the passengers would lean toward that side. There were obviously none of these marvelous Pennsylvania turnpikes on the Cape then. What a relief it was in midwinter when the stage could glide effortlessly into town on runners.

Although the coaches were not described in detail, Henry Kittredge says that Cape coaches were painted gaudy yellows and reds. They were probably the rugged Concord Coaches, made in Concord, N. H., by Leslie Downing and Stephen Abbot. The coach idea came from England but these two young men perfected the stage-coach to be durable first for N. E. and later for the far west. Their coaches were decorated by John Burgun whose talent with bright colors was so apparent, that he was made Chief Ornamentor. These coaches must have been an imposing sight, as drawn by two horses, they traversed the Cape. Sometimes, when many seamen were returning or leaving the Cape, four horses were used, and residents would turn out to see the sight.

Stagecoaches were on the Cape scene a comparatively short time. The iron monsters on the railroad tracks soon took away their business. By the 1880's most passenger, mail and freight traffic was by rail. The last known line was operated by the veteran "whips" Nickerson and Howes. They served the Chatham public with coaches and philosophy until the Chatham railroad spur was built in 1887.

THE INDUSTRY THAT VANISHED

A blank stare is the usual response of today's Cape Codder to the question "Do you have any information about the old fulling mills?" Yet in the early days over one thousand fulling mills energetically processed woolen cloth beside New England streams and at least four of these were on Cape Cod!

Fulling mills were as essential as grist mills to the early colonists. It was proof of a town's progress when it could carry on all the steps of the cloth industry. Brother Johnson in his book "Wonder Working Providence" tells with pride that "by 1654 New Englanders have a fulling mill and cause their little ones to be very diligent in spinning cotton-wool." Wool woven on home looms was considered not presentable until roughly handled by the fuller, who must tread and beat the material to cleanse it of grease and soil then shrink it to a firmer and softer weave. With the rapidly increasing population and the vigors of the New England climate, the demand for woolen garments was unending. Thus fulling mills were necessary to process the cloth woven by the housewives of each village. The material was then speedily returned for cutting and sewing. No wonder Judge Samuel Sewall in his diary exulted when "Brother Moody started a successful fulling mill in Boston" says Alice Morse Earle in her book "Home Life in Colonial Days."

The very first fulling mill was built in Rowley, Mass., in 1643, followed by one in Scituate in 1653. Then Plymouth built one in 1672. As usual Cape Codders were close behind, for in 1689 the first Cape fulling mill was erected in Marstons Mills — then called by its Indian name Misteake. Thomas Marcy (or Massey) was keeper, being granted this privilege with the understanding that he must run it at least 20 years. This he did and more.

Benjamin Marston of Salem appears to be the second operator of a fulling mill in this little village, for the Marston Geneology published by Nathan Washington Marston in 1888 said "Benjamin married Lydia Goodspeed of Barnstable in 1716 and settled there for life. He built the grist mill and also a mill for carding wool and fulling cloth." The Amos Otis papers record that Benjamin Marston "devoted himself to dressing the fabrics of those who brought to his establishment the products of their wheels and looms." The village had taken the name of Goodspeed, but it soon became known as Marstons Mills for a flourishing village grew around the two mills. Benjamin Marston, Jr., succeeded his father in the management of the mills, then Benjamin Jr.'s son Isaiah carried on until the mill burned around 1800. The mill was replaced and operated for a half a century more. Nat Hinckley was the last operator. He was a solid citizen who had a constant feud with the town to idemnify him for damage to his mill rights when water was diverted to cranberry bogs. It is generally thought that the fulling mill was located near the old grist mill site where Routes 28 and 149 meet, but it now appears that the fulling mill site was about half a mile up the river where River Road and Lovell's Lane come together.

The number of fulling mills on Cape Cod is an interesting subject. There is very little recorded anywhere about this early industry. Falmouth had one apparently, for in Cape Cod and the Old Colony author Albert Perry Bingham says "In Falmouth there were eight mills, one a fulling mill." West Yarmouth must have had one, for an old will mentions fulling equipment being left by Miller Baxter to his sons. Sandwich had one, for the Geneology of the Nye Family published in 1907 says that "in August 8, 1675 it was voted that Benjamin Nye have permission to build a fulling mill upon Spring Hill River, providing it does not damifie the county road, and to keep a mill in said place as long as he keeps fulling."

In Brewster a fulling mill was erected near the grist mill at a very early date. It eventually passed into the hands of Kenelm Winslow and was burnt to the ground on February 24, 1769, consuming an estimated one thousand pounds worth of cloth which had been left there by people in various parts of the county. In 1814 a company of eight men started a woolen mill in connection with the old fulling mill, but it was not successful, only operating a few years.

There was another fulling mill just off the Cape at Wareham on the site of the Parker Mills. In 1796 Rev. Noble Everett was granted a lease of water privilege to erect a fulling mill. This mill was operated by the minister and his sons until 1819.

There should be more information about Cape fulling mills soon, because Mr. James Hipper, Curator of the Merrimack Valley Textile Museum in North Andover, is spending many painstaking hours in the archives of the State House viewing microfilms of early industrial Massachusetts maps. As the result of a Commonwealth edict of 1795 each town drew a map of its area, locating its industries. So far Mr. Hipper has located none on Cape Cod, but he has many many more maps to check.

The process of fulling is quite fascinating. A definition reads "Fulling is the process of cleansing, shrinking and thickening cloth by moisture, heat and pressure." Before the advent of mills this was done by foot in tubs and baskets at the edge of streams. At the fascinating Slater Mill Museum in Pawtucket, there is a charming picture of young girls holding their skirts high while they stamp cloth in a woven basket which rests in a flowing stream. Marion Nicholl Rawson in her book "Little Old Mills" says cloth which came from the weaver was not nice to wear until it had been fulled under foot or in the fulling stocks. This almost parallels words written in 1360 in the poem "Vision of the Pers Ploughman". Translated from early English it reads: "Cloth that came from weaving was not comely to wear until it was fulled under foot or in fulling stocks, washed well with water, scratched and dressed with teasels, dyed, tented and put in tailor's hands." This is a very accurate description of the fulling process as it took place in the early American mills.

Housewives brought their cloth to the mill, placing it in separate, labelled bins, for it would never do for the fuller to send someone else's work home to a lady. This loosely woven cloth was placed in a box shaped well. Hot water, soap and fullers earth were added. This latter was a soft gray clay powder originally produced in England, but supplied from Florida in later years. Stocks (sometimes called pestles, stompers, or mallets) were moved back and forth in horizontal positions by water power. They knocked against the cloth, pushing and rolling it. The action of the abrasive and the movement of air pressing through the cloth not only cleansed the material of its

animal grease and soil, but made the fibers shrink length-wise and expand or "blossom" sideways. This created a firm, felt-like surface. The cloth lost its "thready" look and acquired a pleasing softness.

Fulling mills were built in the open country, for the fullers next step was to stretch the cloth taut on tenter-hooks (handwrought iron nails bent like hooks), until it dried. Now we know what it really means to be on tenter-hooks! Next the cloth was "burled" by having the knots and loose threads removed. Finally a good nap was raised on the material with that humble little brown cousin of the thistle, the teasel. This biennial plant is also known as the "fullers thistle". It is said that no modern machine has surpassed the dried flower head of the prickly teasel to raise soft nap, yet not damage the goods. A fine field of teasels was part of the fullers fortune as well as a beau-tiful sight around his mill.

Fulling is done today in the large commercial woolen factories though the process is mechanized. It is also done on a small way here on Cape Cod. A visitor to the Black's weaving establishment on Route 6A in West Barnstable can catch a glimpse of this ancient activity. One of the weavers, Robert R. Black, Jr., has an ingenious fulling tub of his own creation in which to process the woolen mate-rial made on the large floor looms. In a little shed near the shop, he has used an old glass lined fish tank for his tub. His set of 3 stocks were created by electrifying an automobile crankshaft. These pummel and tread upon the material as long or short a time as he desires. This craftsman is very knowledgeable about the old fulling process as well as commercial methods of today, since his advanced college work was in this field.

This long ago industry has been sinking into oblivion. Before all records are gone, there is interest in collecting and preserving information about fulling. A model of early fulling stocks is on exhibition at the North Andover museum, and soon we can see there a Massachusetts map locating all these old mills.

Mr. John Curtis of Old Sturbridge Village confirms that a wool carding mill is being reconstructed in this early American village. As yet the staff has not found an old fulling mill to restore. They would rather refurbish an actual mill rather than create one. We hope Old Sturbridge will rescue this old-time industry from near oblivion.

ARE THEY LOGS OR FISH?

The superior advantages of Cape Cod for fishing were noted by the sharp eyed Pilgrim Fathers in 1620. Ever since this activity has been a "perpetual though varying fountain of wealth" writes the historian Simeon Deyo. Codfish and the Cape were associated long before the Pilgrims, though. Captain Bartholomew Gosnold had an inkling of things to come on May 15, 1602, when his ship's journalist recorded, "Near this Cape we came to anchor in 15 fathoms, where we took great store of codfish, for which we altered the name, calling it Cape Cod." Gabriel Archer, Captain Gosnold's scribe was the first of legions of authors to write about fishing and Cape Cod; the most famous of these was probably Henry David Thoreau.

In 1622 words about fishing were more legal than literary. The Plymouth Company complained to the King of England that 37 English ships were fishing in coastal waters. Whereupon His Majesty decreed all fishing prohibited except by license from the Council of Plymouth. The right to control this industry was the first franchise given the new colony. It also meant the beginning of a permanent and profitable enterprise, since codfish was one of the world's staple foods, and Cape Codders were nearest to the fishing grounds.

Natives climbed into their shallops, dories and schooners throwing out their lines for mackerel, bluefish, haddock or anything edible, but the most picturesque and profitable of the fishing enterprises has always been the chase for the codfish. Although all Cape men fished, Provincetowners seemed to lead the rest, especially in the race for the cod. In the 1850's there were sometimes as many as 100 sails of fishing vessels riding at anchor in Provincetown, while the vessels were being fitted out for the trip to the Grand Banks. The ships usually left the harbor in April to spend 3-5 months at sea.

The reminiscences of Captain Joshua Taylor of Orleans in his "Sea Yarns of a Yankee Shipper" give a vivid picture of a fishing schooner in action. While a young boy, Captain Taylor made his first voyage as a cook aboard the "Pennsylvania" in the year 1850. The ship had its final fitting in Boston, then stopped in Provincetown long enough to pick up 50 barrels of fresh water and chock up with wood. Then she steered eastward the 900 miles to the Grand Banks. On the seventh day out of Cape Cod, the Captain judged by the soundings that they had reached the fishing grounds. The lines were thrown out and there was an immediate bite. Up came a pair of codfish weighing ten pounds each, so the fishing watches began.

Five men fished at a time, each tending two lines having two hooks each. Beside each man was a deck-kid or box into which he heaved the fish as fast as he could haul them in. Every two hours the watch was changed, then each man's catch was counted. The fish were then dumped into the main deck-kid or dressing bin. Here the fish were cleaned and prepared for salting. First one man cleaned the fish, while another took out the backbone and tossed it into a tub of water. When the fish were sufficiently clean, it was the cook's job to toss the fish down the hold to the salter who saw that they were properly salted and stored. The fish usually stopped biting at sun down and the Captain then recorded the number each man caught.

The crewman who caught the most was called the "high-liner" and was much sought after by ship owners. It was tedious, smelly work, and the food was monotonous, but when the schooner turned homeward with 800 quintals or 80,000 pounds of fish, the crew knew their salary was in sight. Young Taylor received for his pay the magnificent sum of 45 dollars for the season plus 50 cents for every hundred codfish he caught.

The process of "making" the fish began when the schooners returned to port with their cargoes. Every man who owned a share came to keep an eye on his bank account. Making the fish consisted of washing it at flood tide as quantities were lifted out in dory loads to the waiting men who stood hip deep in the water. This was called Tide Work. Then the fish were stacked on flakes (racks) to dry.

We are indebted to Thoreau for a description of this process. "Salt fish were stacked up on the wharves looking like cord wood, maple and yellow birch with the bark left on. I mistook them for this at first and such in a sense they were — fuel to maintain our vital fires — an eastern wood which grew on the Grand Banks. Some were stacked in the form of huge flower pots, being laid in a small circle with tail outward, each circle successively larger than the preceding until the pile was three or four feet high, when the circles rapidly diminishd so as to form a conical roof."

Thoreau then describes the fish flakes that cover every available space in the village. "A great many houses were surrounded by fish flakes close to the sills on all sides with only a narrow passage two or three feet wide to the front door. So instead of looking out into flower pots or into a flower or grass plot, you looked into so many square rods of codfish turned wrong side outwards. These were said to be least like a flower garden on a good drying day in mid-summer!"

Thoreau comments that there were flakes of every age and pattern, some so rusty and covered with lichen that they looked as if they might have served the founders of the fish industry. Some had broken down with the weight of the successive harvests."

We can get some idea of the importance of this industry a century ago by looking at statistics in Deyo's history. In 1840 Massachusetts produced half of all fish products in the United States. In 1888 Provincetown, which accounted for one third of all Cape fishing, had 57 vessels usually each manned by 25 men An owner would expect to get 200 quintal (or 200,000 lbs.) of fish for each man employed.

A crew man on a schooner was satisfied to arrive home with a good catch, but he was also looking forward to another reward, the "Fisherman's Dinner". In the old Cape Cod Magazine this is referred to as "a great pleasure recalled by older inhabitants but little known now". It was the custom for those who had shares in each vessel to entertain the crew at this dinner. The food was not fancy but very wholesome and especially welcome after long months at sea. The men responded to the call of the dinner bell still dressed in oil clothes and rubber boots. On this occasion the name of the high liner was released as well as the total of the catch given. The spirit that developed at these dinners often caused men to sign on for another year.

There are countless other tales of fishing that might be told. The Cape Codders chased the mackerel north from the Chesapeake each spring until they reached the Bay of

Fundy in the summer. Then the fishermen followed the leaping schools of mackerel down to Block Island until it was time to go back to the Cape for the winter. Then one year the merry mackerel disappeared to some other part of the world dealing a low blow to the Cape economy. Not till 10 years later did the fish reappear, resuming their northward trip — right into the welcoming hands of the Cape Cod fishermen.

Tales of the herring could be told, not to speak of the lobstering, clamming, etc. Yet here we are concerned with the fishing methods of long ago that were so picturesque and basic to the economy of the towns and the individuals.

Modern inventions and advances in transportation have brought changes. Fishing is still basic to the economy, but one has to go to the harbors and search it out, rather than be surrounded by it in every village. Now fish can be caught one day and served in restaurants in our large cities in a matter of hours, thanks to refrigerated ships and planes. "Making" the fish is no longer necessary, since large cold storage and freezer plants have been built. In the old days of handlining, a 15 year old boy could catch as much fish as his father, but shooting seine and pulling a trawl was another matter.

Thus Henry Kittredge in "Cape Cod its People and its History" says "the rising generation instead of being headed for a career with codfish or mackerel began to seek their fortunes elsewhere." Many Cape Codders coiled their lines and took less appealing but more financially rewarding jobs and another colorful (and odorous) industry no longer lined Cape Cod shores.

WHEN FARMERS WERE WHALERS

The word whaling usually reminds people of huge vessels ranging the seven seas on voyages of long duration. The truth is that the first Cape Codders to profit from catching whales never left the close vicinity of their own shores. Though many Cape men went to sea on whaling ships, most residents did their whaling on the nearest beach. Moreover the white men were not the pioneers of off-shore whaling, the red men did it first.

The records of the first white men to explore the north eastern coast of the United States show that Indian whalers were at work then. In every clan and tribe along the coast there were men renowned for killing whales. One wonders why, though, when their weapons were stone arrowheads and stone headed spears, and they chased their quarry in canoes made of bark, tied together with sinews, and caulked with animal fat and spruce gum. The Indians hunted two kinds of whales. The blackfish were the most common, for they came in large schools to the sheltered waters of Cape Cod. The right whales were less common but much prized. These tremendous objects swam with lips up and open wide, sucking food that floated on the sea. One early historian described the right whale thus: "His head is the third part of him, his mouth (O Hellish wide!) is 16 feet in opening." John Spears in his History of New England Whalers tells us that this sight was so fearsome that later "officers on whale fisheries of the white men were careful never to allow a green horn to look at it lest he be frightened out of his senses." The superstitious Indians with their frail implements must have been exceedingly ingenious and courageous to persevere against these monsters.

Frederick Freeman a Cape historian wrote in 1869 that the Indian method of off-shore whaling was similar to that used by the early colonists, "the fashion being only slightly altered in two centuries." We are indebted to an earlier historian Purchase for a description of the Indian method. In his early 17th century folio "Pilgrimage", he tells us the Indians made floats of logs, using light wood. These floats were attached to stone harpoons by means of short ropes. When a whale was sighted, the Indians leaped into their canoes and gathered around their victim in large numbers, thrusting in their harpoons. Only the strongest whales escaped. The rest expired and, held up by the floats, were towed to shore by two or three canoes.

Whales were plentiful along the shore in the early 1600's. Captain Jones of the Mayflower was tantalized by a school which played around his ship as it lay at anchor in Provincetown. To his chagrin, he had no harpoons. Some Pilgrims immediately wanted to settle on that shore because of the abundance of whales.

Another early traveler, Richard Mather, noted in his journal in 1635 "mighty whales spewing up water in the air like smoke of a chimney, and making the sea about them white and hoary . . . of such incredible bigness that I will never wonder that the body of Jonah could be in the belly of a whale."

Barnstable's first white settlers were farmers not fishermen, records Trayser in Barnstable, Three Centuries a

Cape Cod Town. In the early years these folks thankfully took the "whales old Neptune cast on their beaches, but sought no further". Oil from these drift whales was much in demand, and a welcome supplement to the early economy. These drift whales were so prized that numerous disputes arose over the ownership of this manna from the sea. Legally, these creatures beyonged to the crown. Plymouth colony wanted its slice, however, and naturally the Cape Codders felt finders were keepers. They weren't inclined to share their spoils with colony or crown. In 1651 Constant Southworth, treasurer of the General Court in Plymouth had his eye on the revenue escaping the colony treasury. He sent a proposition for sharing the proceeds from drift whales to the towns of Eastham, Sandwich, Barnstable and Yarmouth. "Loving friends," he wrote, "if you will duly and trewly pay to the countrey for every whale that shall come, one hogshead of oyle at Boston where I shall appoint, and that current and merchantable, without any charge or trouble to the countrey, I say, for peace and quietness sake you shall have it." (The whale) His offer was accepted and an agrement was made for "two Bbls of oyle from each whale . . . to end all troubles". Apparently this didn't end all troubles, though, for in 1690 arbitration was needed. The General Court appointed "to view and inspect whales" Mr. Skiff of Sandwich and Captain Lothrop of Barnstable. The court also passed "an order to prevent contests and suits by whale killers".

The crown was less fortunate than the colony in getting revenue from drift whales. William Clapp, an early resident had great loyalty to his king. He wrote his majesty asking for a warrant to prize drift whales saying, "If I had the power I could have seized several each year for your majesty." Although he was appointed "Water Bayliff" by the king, there is no record that he was very successful in claiming whales for the crown.

To add to the confusion, each town passed its own laws regarding drift whales. Eastham and Truro decided these were blessings sent by the grace of God, so dedicated a part of each find to pay the minister, says Henry Kittredge in Cape Cod, its People and their History. Drift whales did not satisfy the colonists for long. They soon realized that there was wealth swimming all about them and they'd better launch their boats and go after it. Brandishing pitchforks and lances, they followed the Indian's example and went whaling in nearby waters. They were beginning to fulfill the prophecy of an early Nantucket resident who pointed to a school of whales playing off shore and said "Here is a pasture where our children's grandchildren will go for bread."

Whales were most plentiful in Cape waters during the fall and early winter. Since these were lean months for farmers, men turned out for whaling in large numbers. Watches were arranged at lookout stations built on the highest points along the beaches. These shelters were three sided, open toward the sea and had a lookout perch or crows nest. The men lived in "ye whale house", permanent structures with bunkrooms and kitchens. When a watchman spotted a whale's spout or the rounded backs of blackfish, the cry "Whale in the Bay" rang out. The whaling farmers would then put to sea and surround the whales in a fan like line. They would slowly close in yelling and splashing the water with the flat side of their oars. The whales were driven toward shore where they made fine targts and were soon killed. The carcasses were drawn up on shore with heavy tackle rigged to a capstan. Then the blubber was cut off and boiled in the try-yards.

Rev. John Mellen, author of an early historical sketch on Barnstable noted in 1794 that "seventy or eighty years ago the whale bay fishery was carried on in boats from the shore to great advantage. This business employed nearly two hundred men for three months of the year in the fall and beginning of winter." On Sandy Neck in Barnstable there were four try yards. The Proprietors took great care through the years to see that each had a half acre reserved and that cartways and easy access were maintained to the try works. The younger men found farming dull by comparison and each fall were happy to exchange the plough for the lance. In fact Captain John Thatcher had a hard time filling his draft quota during the French and Indian wars because the young bloods were all shore whaling.

Small boys took note of this whaling process too. The story is told of one Truro lad who abandoned some cows he was driving to pasture when he saw a small fish of the whale family floundering on the flats. He rushed out unaided and held it by the tail until the waters receded. Then he killed his quarry with his knife and stripped off the blubber like a professional.

The blackfish was a special prize during these years, for in addition to the blubber and the whalebone, this fish had a "melon" in its head which contained a very special oil. When properly tried out this oil was worth sixty dollars a gallon.

A few years of this type of whaling must have frightened these sea monsters for they stopped coming into the bay. By the middle of the 18th century only an occasional whale was sighted. By this time many Cape residents depended on off-shore whaling for a living, so this was a calamity. The Cape Codders were faced with a decision.

Some, largely from Provincetown, Truro and Wellfleet, took up the challenge of long range whaling and outfitted vessels for long months at sea. Most Cape Codders turned back to the land to earn a living and the leadership of the whaling days was handed over to Nantucket and New Bedford.

Once in a great while nowadays, a whale is stranded on a Cape beach. No longer is it there because it was gamboling too close to the beach. Usually it has been driven to low water by the Killer Sharks. The news "Whale in the Bay" brings Cape residents from all over the peninsular to see this rare sight, once so familiar to the first red and white residents of Cape Cod.

GOLD STRIKE IN THE BOGS

Many century old Cape Cod occupations are now non-existent. Not so with the cranberry industry. In the beginning the process was slightly different and the end result not quite as sweet, but nevertheless the tiny tart berry persists as a basic factor in the Cape economy.

One of the first historical references to the cranberry was in 1677 when a present of ten barrels was sent to King Charles the Second of England. Without an abundance of sugar, the acid tang of the little fruit was not appreciated, so no more were shipped to the mother ocuntry.

According to an Agricultural Bulletin written by Carl Fellers and published in 1930, cranberries grew wild when the Pilgrims landed. This fruit was a staple of the Indian diet. The natives stored them both fresh and dried for winter use. The early settlers watched the Indians collecting their winter supply each October and naturally did the same. One authority claims these berries were named by these same early residents who watched the cranes enjoying them and called them craneberries. It wasn't until almost two hundred years after the landing of the Pilgrims that sugar became readily available and these berries were eaten with enthusiasm. About this time an observing Cape Cod resident is credited with starting the first bog.

In 1816 Henry Hall, who owned a low wet pasture near the beach in Dennis, noticed that sand had drifted over his wild cranberry vines. Mr. Hall expected the vines to die, but to his surprise, he noted that the vines thrived under the blanket of sand, producing larger berries. Intrigued with this development, he experimented with few more square feet with sand, and vines, consistently producing larger and finer berries. This news spread to the neighboring farms and William Sears and his father Elkanah set some vines for their own use. Neighboring Harwich wasn't going to be left out of this. Though Benjamin Bea of that town was quoted as saying "No common use was thought of for these berries," Isaiah Baker set a few square rods before the year 1840. In 1847 Cyrus Cahoon set one-quarter of an acre, no doubt inspired by seeing Henry Hall's process. About this time white sugar became plentiful and the cranberry could be properly sweetened. These propitious circumstances launched an industry that upset the school schedule, provided a social season for the residents, started currency flowing toward the narrow land and made Cape Cod famous the world over.

One of the first to profit from cranberries was Nathan Smith who had gone west to strike gold and had returned empty handed. Back home he found gold in the little red berry and was soon producing enough to hire 50 pickers when harvest time came. His needs were so great that the school system was completely disrupted. This was being felt by all Cape schools. In 1872 the Provincetown Schoolmaster reported in the Town Book that "35 permits were granted to absentees — a large proportion cranberry pickers. Some parents felt the need of assistance of all their children." The schoolmaster's displeasure was evident for he continued "the amount has been a trifling sum when the extra expense of clothing needed for picking was considered. One week 70 cents, another 50 cents. The injury done the children, the mortification they suffer caused by losing their position in class is of tenfold greater hindrance then the benefits derived from the money earned." It was a losing fight, however, for history records that the School officials knew when to compromise. They couldn't afford to pay a teacher to instruct a handful of pupils so the school calendars were changed. School opened the third week in August, continued for five weeks, after which vacation was declared until after cranberry time.

When harvest time came whole families went picking. Cranberry time was eagerly awaited because it was a welcome change from the routine. Not only fathers and school children picked, but women left their washing and ironing to join the throng. Toddlers and grandparents also went along. Wagons stopped at the farmhouses to pick up the workers, then disgorged them at the colorful bogs. Strips of white cloth divided the land into columns, making it look like a track meet. The pickers wrapped cloths around their fingers and wore coverings up over the elbows to prevent being scratched by the vines. Denim aprons with oilcloth patches and oilcloth knee patches for the men protected the workers from the wet soil. Sunbonnets and straw hats (called Sundowns) gave protection from the sun. Races were held to determine the champion pickers. The workers stopped at noon to visit and eat. There was another stop for high tea, then the work went on until sunset. A highlight of the season was the cranberry dance.

The humble cranberry brought a boom to the Cape and money began pouring in. Worthless land became valuable and side industries like box and barrel making thrived. The profits were often one hundred percent and occasionally as high as 134 percent. The mushrooming occupation is illustrated by the following figures: In 1865 barrels numbering 13,324 were produced, while in 1874 production jumped to 44,030 barrels. One of the best years was 1895 when 150,000 barrels were grown, worth one million dollars.

Abel Makepeace of Hyannis — later of West Barnstable and Wareham, was known as the Cranberry King. He brought the business to great heights, importing help from overseas and developing new varieties of the little berry.

The old Atlantic Messenger waxed lyrical over the possibilities of this little fruit for the Cape. "The culture of this fruit is new in the country and there is no danger of the business being overdone. The demand is constantly increasing and Cape Cod cranberries are of superior quality, commanding a premium. For cultivation of this delicious fruit the Cape possesses facilities nowhere else found to the same extent. The expense of the preparation of the land is inconsiderable, land which is valueless for other purposes."

The fame of the Cape cranberry soon spread beyond its borders. Rev. Eastwood of North Dennis wrote a volume on the "Culture of the Cranberry" which found its way to the Jersey shore. Farmers there noted the similarity of their land to the Cape and bought cuttings to start the industry. The news spread across the sea. Cranberry jam, one of the earliest products was sold abroad as early as 1863. William Underwood wrote to Captain Stanwood of the Augusta concerning supplies he had shipped. "Cranberries in bottles, preserved with sugar are to be used precisely as fresh. Any English Man of War you fall in with would add them to the ship's stores. American families will buy them for cabin use." The Cape ship masters took the cranberry around the globe. One ship's record notes that cranberries were sold in India for $1.50 per jar.

An airplane flight over the Cape today will reveal how numerous are the cranberry bogs. In the fall the dark red patches discernible from one end of the Cape to the other are evidence that one industry of a century ago is still going strong today. At Ocean Spray headquarters in Wareham an interesting museum depicts the old industry. Cranberry sherbet, cranberry muffins, and cranberry pancakes are but a few products of the famous red berry, little dreamed of by Henry Hall whose bog now sleeps unworked, having performed its fateful function over a century and a half ago.

IRON FROM THE SWAMPS

Iron smelting suggests vast, glowing blast furnaces in cities like Pittsburgh, Pennsylvania and Gary, Indiana — never Cape Cod. Yet the iron industry once paid the bills and fed the people who lived in the Bourne-Wareham area of the Cape. A reminder is the old Tremont Nail Company in Wareham, which still sells its products throughout the world.

The first settlers of Wareham were farmers and fishermen who had moved down from Plymouth Plantation. In the process of wresting a living from the soil, these first comers cleared the bogs and dredged the swamps. To their amazement, they uncovered deposits of iron ore in the ooze of the wetlands. The iron was found not only in Wareham, but north in Middleboro and Bridgewater. Yankee ingenuity immediately took advantage of these unexpected riches. With visions of new prosperity, the fishermen and farmers turned to pick and shovel, filling wheelbarrows and carts with the ore. They set up crude smelters to separate the precious metal from the residue. Soon they were fashioning many domestic utensils and farm implements which formerly had to be purchased from outside their town.

The deposits of iron ore were a mystery to those early settlers. Now we know, through Barbara Chamberlain's delightful book "These Fragile Outposts" that this low grade spongy ore was a gift from the glacier. By glacial drift, deposits were spread throughout this region, from

Iron Mile Hill in Rhode Island out to Iron Ore Swamp on Martha's Vineyard and on to an iron swamp on Nantucket. These deposits were found particularly in swamps, because they were carried by percolating ground waters as they moved through the soil. Through chemical reaction the iron was redeposited in swampy areas. Occasional deposits occurred throughout the New England-New York area and were mined during the early days. Although the ore was only one-quarter strength, the colonists used it. They couldn't be choosy, especially during the early wars when they needed cannonballs.

The upper and mid-Cape areas had negligible deposits. Various slag piles found near beaches such as Sea Street in Hyannis are reputed to be ballast dumped from ships.

The Wareham chapter of the History of Plymouth County, the Centennial Catalogue published by the Tremont Nail Co. in 1919 and the 200th Anniversary Town Booklet give interesting accounts of the development of the iron industry in that area. After the basic needs of house and farm tools were met, the residents turned to the craft of nail making. It was slow and tedious at first and the volume was small. Gradually the people grew more adept and nearly every home had its furnace and forge. When the output increased, a ready market was waiting out of town. The canny colonists grouped together in neighborhoods and worked cooperatively to increase the volume and to train the children. Finally with the establishment of the Parker Mills in 1819 at the present site of the Tremont Nail Co., nailmaking became a flourishing business.

At first nail cutting was a hand operation. The worker held the metal in a tool while he shaped and pointed the nails. In 1822 Isaac and Jared Pratt of the Parker Mills were operating with a "puddlin furnace" and 50 nail making machines. They took power from the river by raising the level of the water with a 28 foot stone dam. Their works were the finest in America, the old records state, and they traded all over the globe. The Pratts built a rolling mill nearby of which there is now nothing left but a slag heap. Other small mills operated in various sections of the town.

The workers became highly skilled with the new machines as more and more iron went through the huge rollers. Nailers sat on stools in long rows, working with nipping rods in hand as they turned the plate or cut the nails. This was weird to watch especially by torch light as shifts were added around the clock to keep up with the demand.

This industry was of tremendous benefit to the area. Tenements and boarding houses were erected for the workers. Their families overflowed the schools. In the 1850's over 800 children from ages 5-15 filled the schools. There was work for teamsters transporting ore from bog to mills, and for schooners delivering the finished product.

Soon more ore was needed than could be dug locally. With the help of a 200 rod canal dug between the lower pond and the mill as well as the construction of two locks, ore was brought from New Jersey by sea. At the height of the iron industry it was not unusual to see from 11-12 vessels at the wharves at one time discharging ore and loading iron products. Through a series of fires and changes of management as well as the failure of some of the mills, the iron industry persisted, bolstering the local economy.

In 1858 the present Tremont Nail Company came into existence, the lone survivor of the industry. Through the last century of its operation it has made hoops, hollow ware, steel rails, household utensils and all kinds of nails. On the latter is based its present world wide reputation.

There was no planned obsolescence. The Centennial Catalogue states that durability was essential in the old homesteads. Their nails were made to maintain the charming cottages into which they were driven. After a century of service, the Tremont Catalogue boasted, cut nails made a hundred years ago were still faithfully holding together local houses in spite of "trying climactic tests and salt gales that are perennial to this locality".

The iron industry took hold in the Bourne area to a lesser degree. The historian Deyo says the oldest industry in Pocasset was the blast furnace built by Hercules Weston in 1822. Ten years later it became the Pocasset Iron Company and until 1855 it produced stoves, kettles and hollow ware. Another iron works was built in nearby Bournedale. Called the Howard Foundry Company, it rolled iron into plates and cut nails, with ten cutting machines and ten men employed. After several changes of management it was finally turned into a machine shop and foundry. Until 1885 it supplied the Keith Manufacturing Co. in Sagamore with castings.

The early colonists acquired most of this land by purchase from the red men. Three hundred years ago in 1666 four settlers from Plymouth Plantation bought Wareham from seven Indians. Captain Thomas Southworth, Nathanial Warren, William Clark and Hugh Cole, unaware of what was in the swamps and bogs, made quite a bargain for 24 pounds and ten shillings!

FROM METROPOLIS TO GHOST TOWN

In the early 1920's a Sagamore young lady with a brand new license never drove through town at 5 o'clock. She was fearful of the traffic snarl caused by the whistle of the Keith Car & Manufacturing Company when it signalled the exodus of hundreds of mill workers who clogged the streets for miles. This largest of Cape industries, which existed for about one hundred years, created at its peak such a smoke and clatter that it surprised the tourist, commented historian Albert Brigham. Cape visitors expected peace and harmony, but instead when they entered the Cape they couldn't see the Bay through the endless chain of new and empty freight cars that stood on the siding leading to Sandwich.

Historians differ on the exact beginnings of the car works. Some place it as early as 1826-29 when Isaac Keith in partnership with a man named Ryder, began shoeing horses and building carts, wagons, sleighs and wheelbarrows. Their shop site was by an old mill dam which the Indians called Scusset and the settlers called West Sandwich, but later renamed Sagamore. A resident who interviewed Mr. and Mrs. Eben Keith in 1923 placed the beginnings of the company in 1846 when Isaac Keith began manufacturing carriages under the name of Keith and Ryder. Soon stagecoaches were built and then prairie schooners. Agnes Edwards in "Cape Cod New and Old" says the most notable of their prairie schooners which traveled the western deserts in 1849 was Captain Sutter's when he "sallied forth to find his spctacular fortune of gold". At this time tools were also manufactured by Keith & Ryder for the California mines.

The railroad arrived in Sandwich in 1848 with a stop arranged especially for a neighboring industry the Sandwich Glass Company. Keith & Ryder took advantage of this, finding a ready market for a new product — freight cars. Production was stepped up by using the railroad to import materials and export products. One of the earliest cars was of Keith's own design — a small one made to carry sand or coal.

Sons Hiram T. Keith and Isaac N. Keith worked with their father, finally purchasing the business in 1869 just prior to the founder's death. At this point the name of Ryder disappears. By 1882 Isaac N. Keith became the sole owner and began constructing more buildings for the rapidly expanding business.

Isaac's son, Eben Smith Sturgis Keith, born in 1872, grew up amidst the excitement of the large manufacturing plant. After graduating from Bourne High School, he went to work with his father. His twenty-eighth year marked two turning points in his life as well as the entrance into the next century. In 1900 he married Miss Malvina Landers of Cotuit, a Bourne school teacher, and at the death of his father, the entire responsibility for the plant rested on his shoulders. About this time the cavernous paint shop was constructed, rising several stories high and topped by a truss roof.

The plant was enlarged again in 1907 when it became a subsidiary of the Standard Steel Car Company of Pittsburgh. At this time Charles Streicher came to be manager of the works. Further prominence came to the company at the end of the decade with the building of the Cape

Cod Canal. By this time the specialty of the plant was freight cars and it had become the largest manufacturer of them in New England.

In the book "Building of the Cape Cod Canal" by Reid, edited by Amussen, we are told that the excavated material was sold to the Keith Manufacturing Company for its expanding plant. The book also notes the inconveniences caused by the canal to the residents, for their villages were cut in half. This was true in Sagamore and Bournedale where residents lived on one side and their jobs at the car works were on the other.

In spite of such difficulties the business continued to grow, reaching its peak of production and employment in 1918 when the weekly payroll was $25,000. At this time the plant was immense and sprawling, its buildings extending over a mile. It had 25 acres of factory floor space and employed about 1200 people. Though the average output was 20 cars a day, one present day resident recalls his father coming home to announce the record output of 27!

An embryo freight car began in the Truck and Underframe building (which stood quite close to the eastern end of the present Sagamore Bridge). The assembly line rolled the car on to the Carpenter Shop and the combination Blacksmith-Machine Shop. Each car was finished at the Paint Shop, which was largest of all, then rolled out onto the railroad siding. The finished cars were shipped immediately. Many a small Sagamore boy came home at night with tell tale paint on his clothes; but what small boy could resist climbing under the board fence to see the fascinating sights of the car works, and go swimming in the canal beyond.

Other buildings in the vast plant were: the power plant, office headquarters, the mammoth elevated hydrant tank with its capacity of 225,000 gallons, a fire station housing two fire pumps capable of throwing 1000 gallons of water per minute, two storehouses, a general store annexed to the paint shop, and the oil house where 6 kinds of oil were kept including sperm oil for the hydraulic press. In addition there were four large tenement buildings for the many Italian families who came from Italy — some directly and some by way of the Plymouth Cordage Company. There was also the business block on Main Street built in 1908 and torn down in 1966.

The effects of the industry on the town were tremendous. With cars going overseas, there was international interest. During World War I France ordered 40,000 cars. About half the size of American freight cars, they were called 40 and 8's (designed to carry forty men and eight horses). The growth of the car works caused over crowding in the schools. Sagamore condemned its two room schoolhouse and erected an up-to-date building housing 250 pupils. The business catupulted its owner into politics as it did his father before him. In 1906 Eben Keith was elected a State Senator and was later a member of the Governor's Council during the term of Governor Foss. Now the Honorable Eben S. S. Keith, he was following in his father's footsteps, for Isaac Keith had also been a State Senator and member of the Governor's Council. Eben Keith was in addition several times a delegate to Republican National Conventions.

Former employees like Bruce Jerould and Fred Burrows remember Eben Keith as a very sociable, gregarious person having a "personal touch" with his workers. It was said of him that he could walk into the office of any railroad president in the eastern part of the United States without knocking! Then, when he returned from such a visit, he would walk through the factory, visiting with the men, inquiring by name about their wives and children.

In the 1920's the company stopped building new freight cars. Instead the workers repaired cars for the New York, New Haven and Hartford line. The steel mills now could make new freight cars far cheaper, using metal bodies. Originally pine lumber was secured from the Virginias and Carolinas. Now fir had to be brought by ship from the west coast, unloaded onto gondola cars and sent by special train to Sagamore. A victim of declining markets and rising costs, the enterprise fluctuated in volume, adding workers when a large order came in and dropping them in slack times. Another factor that did not help was the illness of Mr. Keith. His health worsened and he eventually was not active in the business at all.

In 1928 when the Pullman Company and the Standard Steel Car Company merged, all subsidiary companies were involved including the Sagamore plant, and many workers were let go. The car works finally ground to a halt in 1930 when the skeleton crew then operating the plant received notice the plant would close in a week's time. A dismantling crew stayed into 1931. In 1932 the federal government, new owners of the property, tore down some of the now vacant buildings when it widened the Cape Cod Canal. Mr. Keith lived on in ill health until 1935. Mrs. Keith remained in the Keith home in Sagamore until her death in 1966, a kind and generous person also, affectionately remembered by her Sagamore neighbors.

Sagamore has reverted to a quiet village, except when summer people come. Long time residents refer to it as a ghost town, comparing it with the activity of fifty years ago. Reminders of the old days come now and then. When workers constructed the new hydro-electric plant near the Sagamore-Sandwich border, they dug up some contour shaped amber bricks. These turned out to be from the ruins of the old tower of the Keith car works. A new industry, like the Phoenix of old, is rising where another perished.

KEEPERS OF THE ORDINARY!

Innkeepers have been operating on Cape Cod ever since the Pilgrim days, though the percentage was nowhere near as great as it is today. Dutch traders, Governor Bradford's Plantation officials, and Myles Standish's soldiers needed places to stay on their travels, so the first Innkeepers were licensed to "keep Ordinarys" as Inns were then called.

The first detailed Innkeeper's permit appears in the old Plymouth Scrapbook, which is a collection of deeds, wills and notices of the early Plymouth Colony. Dated 1664, the permit reads "This court doth discharge Joseph Barstow from keeping of an ordinary and doth grant Lycense unto Joseph Sylvester to keep an ordinary at his house at North River for the entertainment of Strangers, to be well provided with the necessities for the entertainment both for them and their horses in respect to good diet and bedding. Also, that he keep good order in his house, that he incur no just blame through his neglect."

Many of those early travelers traversed the Cape. Though the name of Cape Cod's first Innkeeper is lost among fragmented records, we know that Anthony Thatcher was the first "keeper of an ordinary" in Yarmouth, being authorized to "draw wine" in 1644, while John Crocker got his license in Barnstable in 1649. These first licenses were merely permits to lodge people at Innkeeper's homes and sell them food and drink. Colony officials, with fresh memories of thieving European land-

lords, were very careful to license only the most discreet and highly respected citizens. Corruption could easily arise, they reasoned, when travelers must trust themselves, their baggage, their horses and their money to strangers. Therefore, Innkeepers were recommended by the Selectmen and the Sheriffs, then licensed by the General Court. Licenses could be lost if strict rules were not followed, Edward Sturgis of Yarmouth, for example, lost his license in 1663 for bringing too much liquor into town. John Miller was appointed in his place.

For the most part those early Innkeepers and their families treated the travelers with great decency, showing an interest in their happiness and welfare. The Duke de la Rochefoncault fell ill while traveling in Massachusetts. He was nursed back to health by Innkeeper Charles Williams and his family, thus earning the Duke's supreme gratitude. Another energetic traveler who spoke highly of Innkeepers, was Timothy Dwight, President of Yale, who said "In my experience Innkeepers would do everything in their power to contribute to the traveler's relief." Dwight could speak with authority, for he spent his annual six weeks' vacation traveling during the late 1700's. His four journals describing his travels into New England, New York, Canada and Virginia are filled with appreciations and descriptions of Innkeepers. Traveling through Mashpee he writes "The Inn at which we dined was kept by a respectable family who entertained us with great civility and kindness." Earlier he noted "We lodged at Harwich with Captain A. This man had been thirty years at sea, he informed us with great emphasis and had seen the world. Now he was the principal farmer in Harwich." Dwight was the forerunner of other guide book writers, setting himself to the task in order to "set down what it is like to travelers now for curious people a hundred years into the future."

By colonial times Inns were still in private homes, but ells had been added for the travelers. At this time the term ordinary was replaced by the word Inn if lodging and board were dispensed. Tavern was the term used if food and drink were served. There were stables for the comfort of equine guests. Private rooms were unheard of. Locks weren't generally used until much later — around 1840. Colonial lawmakers voted that Inns and Taverns must have swinging signs partly pictorial, since some people did not know how to read, thus all unaware, starting a collector's hobby of today. One old sign read:

> "Pull up your ropes and anchor here
> Till better weather doth appear."

Another said:

> "Pause, Traveler here, just stop and think
> A weary man must need a drink."

A third read:

> "Before you do this hill go up
> Stop and drink a cheery cup."

While the reverse side said:

> "You're down the hill, all danger's past
> Stop and drink a cheerful glass."

Innkeeper's advertising was as enterprising then as now. Dr. Nathanial Ames Sr., in 1751 advertised that he "kept a house of public entertainment eleven miles from Boston at the Sign of the Sun. If they want refreshment and see cause to be my guests, they shall be well entertained at reasonable prices."

Edward Field in his book "The Colonial Tavern" notes the proximity of the village taverns to the meeting houses. Services and town meetings were long. Though sermons and discussions might be hot, the buildings were not for most of the year. The Taverns were purposely located nearby so people could repair to them between and after the meetings for warmth and refreshment. Many an item of town business was finished around tavern tables.

When stagecoaches began to lumber down the Cape, Inns developed into oases for thirsty travelers. There was Fessenden's at Sandwich; Howland's in West Barnstable; then Crocker Tavern in Barnstable Village. Four miles beyond was Sears Tavern in Yarmouth and so on down the Cape to Provincetown. There were ordinaries kept by Widow Knowles and Squire Crowe at Chatham, while Edward Bangs and Daniel Cole were licensed to draw wine in Eastham. On the south side Elisha Nye was the Innkeeper in Falmouth during the Revolution. The list could go on and on, for by this time the resort concept had begun to sprout.

If we don't count the clans of Indians who, previous to the Pilgrims, came to the Cape in season to fish, or Queen Awashonks, ruler of the Narragansetts who summered at Gay Head, the beginnings of the resort era as we know it started in the mid-1800's. This boon to Innkeepers had some early advocates, such as Daniel Webster who put up at the Sandwich Inn, but it was really Henry David Thoreau's book about his Cape Cod hikes that started this area on its path to fame as a vacationland. Thoreau was the first press agent of the outer Cape as he wrote about his four visits that took place between 1849 and 1857. He records visits to Higgins Tavern in Orleans and the Atlantic House as well as the Fuller House in Provincetown.

About this time various church groups summered on the Cape giving rise to another type of Innkeeper. Camp meetings sprang up all over Cape Cod in the 1800's. Each developed Inns to take care of vacationing conferencees. The South Wellfleet Camp Meeting brought Methodists by the thousands by boat and carriage. In 1829 Eastham's Campground was taking the overflow. In 1835 Weslyan Grove on Martha's Vineyard came into existence, followed by the Yarmouth Campground in 1862. Ten years later the Christian denomination chose Craigville for its combination vacation and Camp meeting settlement. Of the many Inns and boarding houses erected, Craigville Inn is still in existence, operated as a conference center by the United Church of Christ. Near where the Cape begins, Bradford Arms and Sagamore Lodge catered to delegates to the Sociological Conferences and the Christian Endeavour movement.

Meanwhile, primitive Cape Inns had developed and improved, influenced by their cousins the city hotels and the better standards of living. At this period Cape Cod was noted for Santuit House in Cotuit, the Falmouth Heights Town Hotel, Cotocheset House in Wianno and Nobscusset House in Dennis. In "Early American Inns and Taverns", Elsie Lathrop mentions the Red Inn of Provincetown and the Truro Hotel. Barnstable Inn, now billed as the Cape's oldest, was well into its first century, having begun in 1799 as Eldridge Tavern. This was the era when Innkeepers were true hosts, dispensing hospitality personally. The success of Cape Cod as a vacationland seemed assured. Simeon Deyo wrote hopefully and prophetically "In summer comes a salubrity of climate, remarkably even temperature and an opportunity for pleasure which brings hundreds of strangers to the Cape each season."

The natives weren't listening, however, for Cape Cod was deep in an economic slump. Folks were moving away to the cities in droves. Old industries like the Sandwich Glass Company had failed, while former occupations like salt making and whaling were non-existent. Even the folks at the State House were worried. A report issued in 1897 painted a gloomy picture. "Native inhabitants are abandoning the land." The population drop in the 16-60 age bracket was serious — two thousand less than ten years previous! A desperate search for new industry was under way, the most promising being "collecting seaweed to make sheathing for deadening sound in lining walls" — the first insulation?

In an offhand manner Harwichport and South Harwich were listed as summer resorts, with Provincetown having possibilities as a watering place! Thus in casual fashion was the Cape's future livelihood set aside, residents little realizing that resorts would soon burst into full bloom bringing the Cape its biggest industry and new life to the occupation of Innkeeping.

THE THREE R'S ON OLD CAPE COD

The job of teacher was not easy a century or two ago on Cape Cod. Ungraded schools, spasmodic schedules plus the lack of buildings and materials must have been discouraging to the early pedagogues. Yet they persisted, bringing education to Cape children almost as soon as the Pilgrims landed.

Education was considered paramount by those first settlers and the school teacher was held in community esteem second only to the minister. Teaching elders were the first educators. These were appointed by the colony in the 1630's. The first Cape teaching elder was probably John Mayo of Barnstable, appointed in 1637 the town's first year. Though primarily responsible for religious instruction, some rudiments of reading and writing were surely taught. Books were prized possessions brought on the Mayflower and subsequent vessels for most of the Pilgrims were people of education and intelligence. It was clear they determined to transmit this heritage to their children.

In 1633 the Colony Court took action to start an education system. It proposed "that some course be taken in every town that there be a schoolmaster set up to train children in reading and writing". Simple education was not enough, however, for Harvard University was founded just eighteen years after the Pilgrims landed. In 1666 school taxes had begun. The fisheries of Cape Cod (then the name for Provincetown) were regulated by law. A duty of twelve pence a barrel was laid on all fish caught to start a school fund. In 1670 this was implemented by the following legislation:

"Such proffets as might or should annually acrew or grow dew to this Collonie from time to time, for fishing with netts or saines att Cape Codd for mackerell, basse or herrings . . . for and toward free scools in some towne of this jurisdiction, for the training up of youth in litterature for the good and benefitt of posteritie."

With this revenue the first school was established at Plymouth. John Morton was the master and Thomas Hinckley of Barnstable the first steward of the fishery money.

Cape Cod natives were not satisfied with one school which benefitted only the children in the town of Plymouth. Along with other towns, they petitioned for a share of the money. In the 1682-3 records we read "This court have ordered the Cape money as followeth, viz: Bastable scoole twelve pound; to Duxborrow Scoole eight pound; to Rehoboth Scoole five pound; to Taunton Scoole three pound . . ." Thus Barnstable had one of the first five schools in the county and received the largest amount of money. Shortly after, in 1687, the Colony Court made it compulsory for towns of fifty or more families to employ a schoolmaster to teach a grammar school. Each township was required to raise twelve pounds among the inhabitants, with those receiving the most benefit paying the most. The balance came from the fishery money.

Early schoolmasters could never get rich. Salaries were exceedingly meager. In 1695 Sandwich appropriated ten pounds a year for the schoolmaster. The pay was still the same in 1699 when the job description read "he to teach reading, writing and arithmetic." The schoolmaster's salary was approximately one-third of the minister's. By 1710 the teacher's salary had doubled "twenty pounds and diet — he to board around". Samuel Jennings was the incumbent then. On an illfated trip to England at the age of nineteen, Samuel had been impressed on board a ship of war. In attempting to escape at a West Indian port, he lost a hand and a foot — bitten off by a shark. The historian Frederick Freeman theorized that, being maimed, he probably devoted himself to a superior education.

By 1712 Sandwich employed two schoolmasters, hiring Samuel Osborne of Edgartown and increasing the salary to twenty-five pounds. Osborne taught Latin and Greek. Parents paid according to the subjects taken by their children. Reading cost 3 shillings per week, writing added 2 shillings, while a combination of the three basics cost 6 shillings per week. Latin and Greek increased the total to eight. The school budget was sometimes difficult to raise. The towns set aside certain land as school property. The income was used for school maintenance. For example in 1702 Squaw Island and the W. Hyannisport area comprised the "scool lot". These acres supplied school funds for a century and a half.

Meanwhile other Cape teachers were struggling on insufficient salaries. Mr. Absom taught the first schools in Harwich for 9 pence a week. In Falmouth young Samuel West taught for twenty pounds a year and board. He was from Yarmouth and was "fitting himself for college by the aid of a few friends and his own industry". Wellfleet, fortunate to secure a Harvard graduate in 1768, appointed John Greenough to keep the grammar school "the scool to be attended by such as to learn the Latin and Greek languages." Another school was arranged for reading, writing and aritluaetic. The teacher was paid the municent sum of forty pounds a year.

The first school marm may have been Hannah Sargent, who didn't rate very high on the salary scale. She was engaged as "school-dame" in Falmouth in 1716 for "twelve pounds and diet a year — only the agents shall obtaine her as much cheaper as they can". Apparently Hannah was aggrieved about something, for she was offered the job in 1718 but refused. "Not succeeding in obtaining the services of Miss Sargent as schoolmistress" the records state Isaac Green and Timothy Robinson were appointed at the next town meeting to find a replacement — at the same price. It seems loneliness was the cause of the unhappiness, for the next schoolmistress accepted at the same salary but with the fringe benefit of the "use of a horse twice a year to visit her friends."

During the first century schoolmasters had no permanent cupboards for their supplies and no schoolhouses. Classes were held in homes, with a rebate for school taxes given to the householders who housed the school. In Barnstable, for example, Nathaniel Bacon was paid 3 shillings rent for housing the school.

No special transportation carried pupils off to school. Instead the master came to the pupils. Teachers taught a few weeks in one section of town, then moved to another, spending the longest period where the pupils were more numerous. In 1732 Barnstable divided the school master's four year contract equally between the two town precincts, casting lots to see which section got him first. The old record reads: "in the East Precinct it shall be each year first near the meetinghouse 42 weeks, and near the new house of Thomas Haddaway 10 weeks; in the West Precinct near John Howland's 33 weeks, near the house of Benjamin Goodspeed's 14 weeks and 3 days and near the house of James Lovel Jr. 4 weeks and 4 days." In Sandwich in the year 1730, school was held "first at Peters Pond 4 months, then at Spring Hill 5 months, the Center 12 months, Scusset 5 months, Pocasset 3 months and Manomet 3 months in succession." One wonders what happened to education in Manomet for example in the 32 intervening months between the arrival and departure of school!

One can pretty much judge the population centers of those days from the town records. In Harwich in 1725 there were six "removes" of the town's floating school. The first had 29 children and lasted 6 months, one week; the second had 55 children and lasted 8 months, 2 weeks; the third remove consisted of 56 children while the term lasted 8 months and 3 weeks; the fourth had 47 children and an 8 month 1 week interval; the fifth had 42 children lasting 4 months; the sixth had 35 children and lasted 6 months, one week. School started at the western part of town and moved eastward with no regard for the calendar year. A bit later all Cape schools were further complicated by a recess during the cranberry season.

The first school building erected on the Cape was built in Barnstable in 1771. On March 7th that year it was voted that "there may be a school house set up on the highway against the old burying place in Barnstable, on the north side."

Those first buildings have been described as about 25 foot square, painted red and having an entry used for wood and clothes. There were two rows of unpainted plank desks and backless seats about 10 feet long. Girls sat on one side and boys the other. A fireplace and the teacher's pine boxlike desk were at the front. The boys gathered the firewood and tended the fire, while the girls kept the school neat. Scholars ranged in age from 8-20.

No materials were supplied then. By town vote parents had to provide their children with books, pens, ink and paper. The schoolmaster was instructed to refuse to accept any pupil whose parents did not supply a proportionate share of wood to warm the school and money to maintain it. The little schoolhouses at Yarmouthport and at the National Seashore Park are reminiscent of this era.

By 1844 Provincetown proudly boasted two schools with improved plans. Each had two stories, with rooms above and below for recitations, these connected with the main rooms and furnished with globes, maps, and various apparatus. These schools were forerunners of the many fine buildings yet to come on Cape Cod.

With the advent of school buildings, the district system evolved. In 1794 Barnstable citizens voted to keep "one good Latin grammar school and four English grammar schools, also to divide the town into 13 districts. The inhabitants of each should provide suitable school building or room." State laws compelled towns to have school committees who inspected and reported back on each district school. Thus the Commonwealth hoped to insure some quality and order among rapidly multiplying schools. The district system was not the best. Sometimes district committees were at odds wih the town committee. More often they were at odds with each other. Teachers however, had more pressing things to worry about.

Discipline was an eternal problem. Many boys were away at sea on fishing fleets all spring and summer, attending school only in winter. Teaching these mature young men their three R's and at the same time starting a flock of youngsters on the pathway to learning was an almost insurmountable task. The Barnstable school committee of 1849 told town meeting that there were "eleven unruly boys in Mrs. Cornish's district who were disposed to be turbulent and disorderly" and suggested the impropriety of employing females to teach school in the winter term. Two women were the exception to this rule. Martha and Eunice Whelden of West Barnstable were "tall, strong and entirely fearless, maintaining high standards of order and thoroughness of instruction". During their 39 years of teaching they were sent from one district to another to set schools to rights. The forms of punishment other masters used to discipline their pupils were many, varied and better left unmentioned.

Despite these dismaying factors, education improved and expanded on Cape Cod. Sandwich Academy was founded in 1803, bringing higher education to Cape pupils. Barnstable's academy in 1835 followed Falmouth's by just one year. Truro Academy was formed in 1840. Private and specialized schools flourished, such as the singing school at Wellfleet. Harwich developed what was probably the first vocational school in the country, with one course quite appropriately being navigation. The highest school was undoubtedly the High School held under the eaves of the Parish Church in West Barnstable, where Robert Samuel taught to earn his way through Dartmouth College.

Through these dedicated pedagogues and these sometimes faulty institutions, and by means of the Horn book, the Bible and the New England Primer, education came to the hearts and minds of those early Cape children, raising up leaders like Governor Thomas Hinckley, Colonel James Otis, "Mad Jack" Percival and Judge Lemuel Shaw.

BIBLIOGRAPHY

GENERAL REFERENCES

Three Centuries a Cape Cod Town by Donald Trayser, 1939.
History of Cape Cod by Frederick Freeman, 1858.
History of Barnstable County by Simeon Deyo, 1890.
Cape Cod, Its People and Their History by Henry Kittredge, 1930.

CHAPTER I

Old Newspaper Clipping by Mrs. B. H. McHenry.

CHAPTER II

Sandwich the Town that Class Built by Harriot Barbour, 1948.
We Chose Cape Cod by Scott Corbett, 1955.

CHAPTER III

Two Men on a Mill by Harold Castonguay, 1962.
The Young Millwright and Miller's Guide by Oliver Evans, 1800.

CHAPTER IV

American Encyclopedia — Water.
Provincetown Advocate Clipping by Gertrude DeWager.

CHAPTER V

Pilgrim Returns to Cape Cod by Edward Rowe Snow, 1946.
Cape Cod Ahoy by Arthur Tarbell, 1932.
When Boston Packet Boats Tied Up by Willar DeLue (clipping).

CHAPTER VI

Cape Cod Yesterdays by Joseph C. Lincoln, 1935.
The Old Post Road by Stewart Holbrook, 1962.
Home Life in Colonial Days by Alice M. Earle, 1900.

CHAPTER VII

Little Old Mills by Marion N. Rawson, 1935.
Cape Cod and the Old Colony by Albert P. Brigham, 1920.
Ancient Landmarks of Plymouth by Davis, 1899.
Amos Otis Papers.
Marston and Nye Geneologies.
Home Life in Colonial Days by Alice M. Earle, 1900.

Chapter VIII

Sea Yarns of a Yankee Skipper by Joshua Taylor (clipping).
Cape Cod Magazine February 1922.
Cape Cod by Henry David Thoreau.

Chapter IX

The American Whaleman by Elmo P. Hohman, 1928.
Cape Cod Facts by Oiver Knowles.
Story of New England Whalers by John R. Spears, 1908.

Chapter X

Cape Cod New and Old by Agnes Edwards, 1918.
Cape Cod a Historical Narrative by Charles Swift, 1847.
Cape Cod Pilot by Jeremy Digges, 1937.
Uncle Seth and Cranberry Time by Geneva Eldridge.
Agricultural Bulletin — Historical Notes by Carl Fellers, 1930.

Chapter XI

History of Plymouth County — Town of Plymouth by William T. Davis.
Centenary Catalogue — Tremont Cut Nails, 1918.
Two Hundredeth Anniversary Program — Wareham, 1939.
These Fragile Outposts by Barbara B. Chamberlain, 1966.

Chapter XII

Cape Cod Old and New by Agnes Edwards, 1918.
Cape Cod and the Old Colony by Albert Bingham, 1920.
Building of Cape Cod Canal (Edited Amussen) by William Reid, 1961.

Chapter XIII

Early American Inns and Taverns by Elise Lathrop, 1926.
Yesterday's Tides by Florence W. Baker, 1941.

Chapter XIV

Cape Cod Old and New by Agnes Edwards, 1918.

INDEX

PAGE

Abel, F. A. 14
Abbott 28
Ames, Dr. Nathanial, Sr. 66
Archer, Gabriel 37
Awashonks, Queen 72
Bacon, Daniel 22
Bacon, Nathanial 73
Bangs, Edward 67
Barnstable Inn 68
Baxter family 12
Bonique, Gaffer 7
Bradford Arms 68
Bradford, William 63
Burgen, John 28
Cahoon, Cyrus 49
Car works 57
Christian Endeavour 68
Clapp, William 44
Clark, Edward 1
Clark, Myrick 2
Clark, William 56
Corn 11
Cornish, Mrs. 76
Cornish, John F. 27
Cole, Hugh 56
Cotocheset House 68
Craigville Camp Meeting 68
Cranberries 48
Crocker, John 63
Crocker Tavern 27, 67
Crosby (miller) 4
Crowe, Squire 67
Downing, Leslie 28
Dwight, Timothy 65
Eastwood, Rev. 51
Eldridge Tavern 68
Everett, Rev. Noble 32
Falmouth Heights Hotel 68
Farris, Reuben 13
Fessenden's Tavern 27
Fishing 37
Fulling mills 30
Glass works 5
Glauber salt 17

PAGE

Goodspeed, Lydia 31
Goodspeed, Benjamin 74
Gosnold, Bartholomew 37
Green, Isaac 73
Greenough, John 72
Haddaway, Thomas 73
Hall, Henry (miller) 12
Hall, Henry 48, 52
Harris, Rice 7
Hatch Tavern 3
Higgins Tavern 67
Hinckley, John 71
Hinckley, Matthias 22
Hinckley, Nathanial 31
Hinckley, Thomas 76
Howard, Charles 27
Howland, John 74
Howland Tavern 27, 67
Huckins, Thomas 20
Innkeeping 63
Iron Works 54
Jarves, Deming 5
Johnson, Brother 30
Jones, Captain 43
Keith Car Works 56, 57
Keith, Eben 57, 58, 60
Keith, Hiram T. 58
Keith, Isaac 57, 58
Kelly, David 14
Kelly, Hallel 17
Kenney, William 14
Knowles, Widow 67
Landers, Malvina 58
Loring, Elisha 23
Lothrop, Captain 44
Lovel, James Jr. 74
Makepeace, Abel 51
Marcy, Thomas 31
Marston, Benjamin 31
Marston, Benjamin, Jr. 31
Marston, Isaiah 31
Mather, Richard 43
Matthews, Thomas 22
Mayo, John 70

INDEX (Continued)

PAGE

Mellen, John 21, 46
Miller, Experience 1
Miller, John 65
Mills 11
Morton, John 71
Nickerson 29
Nobscusset House 68
Nye, Elisha 67
Nye, Benjamin 32
Osborne, Samuel 72
Otis, James 76
Packet Boats 20
Paine, Thomas 11
Percival, "Mad Jack" 76
Percival, Thomas 22
Pratt, Isaac 55
Pratt, Jared 55
Purchase 43
Railroads 2, 24, 28, 29
Red Inn 68
Robinson, Timothy 73
Rochefoncault, Duke de la 65
Ryder 57
Sagamore Lodge 68
Salt Works 15
Samuel, Robert 76
Sandwich Glass 5, 69
Santuit House 68
Sargent 73
School teaching 70
Sears, Elkanah 49
Sears, John 15

PAGE

Sears, Reuben 17
Sears Tavern 28, 67
Sears, William 49
Shaw, Lemuel 76
Skiff 44
Smith, Nathan 49
Southworth, Constant 44
Southworth, Thomas 56
Stagecoaches 25
Standish, Myles 63
Stanwood, Captain 51
Streicher, Charles 58
Sturgis, Edward 65
Sutter 57
Sylvester, Joseph 63
Tanning 1
Taylor, Joshua 38
Teasel 35
Thatcher, Anthony 63
Thatcher, John 46
Truro Hotel 68
Underwood, William 51
Warren, Nathanial 56
Webster, Daniel 8, 67
Weslyan Grove, Martha's Vineyard 68
Weston, Hercules 56
Whaling 42
Whelden, Eunice 76
Whelden, Martha 76
Williams, Charles 65
Yarmouth Campground 68

ABOUT THE AUTHOR

Marion Vuilleumier is a Cape resident, mother of three and wife of a clergyman. She has written extensively on Cape Cod history, is host of the television show Books and the World, and is executive secretary of the Cape Cod Writers' Conference.

Her books are: *Boys and Girls on Olde Cape Cod, Indians on Olde Cape Cod, Sketches of Old Cape Cod, Craigville on Old Cape Cod, Churches on Cape Cod, Along the Wampanoag Trail, America's Religious Treasures, Cape Cod in Color, Martha's Vineyard in Color* and *Meditations By The Sea.*

ABOUT THE ILLUSTRATOR

Louis Edward Vuilleumier, son of Marion, is a graduate of Defiance College in Ohio with an art major. He is proprietor of the New England Art Gallery in Cummaquid which produces carved quarterboard signs and artistic antique slate gifts.